Life Lines

Cover art by Aidan Robertson

Frederick Mundle

Life Lines: Copyright 2024 by Frederick Mundle

All rights reserved. No part of this publication may be reproduced, stored in a retrieval system, or transmitted in any form or by any means, without the prior written consent of the publisher or, in the case of photocopying or other reprographic copying, a license from Access Copyright (Canadian Copyright Licencing Agency).

Published 2024 (ISBN 978-1-0688378-0-7) by CFP Concepts, Inc.

First Printing: JUNE, 2024

Design and in-house editing by F. Mundle

Cover Art by Aidan Robertson

Appreciation is hereby extended to Xenoble
for its total support in producing this book.

For additional information and inquiries:
CFP Concepts, Inc.
8 Jayden Lane, Moncton, NB
E1G 0S2   Canada

To order additional copies of this book, contact:
CFP Concepts, Inc.
506-204-1187
cfpconcepts@live.ca

Library and Archives Canada Cataloguing in Publication Data
Mundle, Frederick Lorne, 1944

CONTENTS

i.   Introduction
ii.   Acknowledgements
iii.   Other Christiani Publications by the Author
iv.   Youtube Addresses for the Author's Christian Songs

Table of Contents

2.	We All Know Where…
4.	Let No Sunset See…
6.	He Who Says Nothing…
8.	Let Kind Words Fly…
10.	A Wagging Tongue…
12.	If You Don't believe…
14.	Pity Those Who Have…
16.	Step on Your Hands
18.	A Real Carpenter…
20.	What You Bare…
22.	If Stones Were Coins…
24.	Better a Skateboard…
26.	The Early Bird…
28.	Every Father Wants to See…
30.	When Stones Turn to…
32.	If Darwin Was Saved…
34.	All His Children…
36.	Sow in the Season…
38.	Where Is Einstein…

40.	You are not a fisherman until…
42.	If you can still count your works…
44.	People Without God...
46.	You Are Not a Farmer Until…
48.	Many a Rock…
50.	Only a Christian is…
52.	Christian Prayers are…
54.	Mute Christians Will Answer…
56.	The Pagan Lives for…
58.	Bad News for…
60.	Non-Christians Have Nothing…
62.	No Matter what…
64.	A Christian Has…
66.	A Christian always looks…
68.	The World Is a Bootcamp for…
70.	Let the Heathen Have…
72.	Stored Treasures in Heaven…
74.	If You Don't Know Jesus…
76.	Jesus Is the Only…
78.	Bet Your life on…
80.	Jesus Hires Anybody…
82.	It's Too Late When…
84.	If Jesus Is the Light…
86.	If You Give Your Heart…
88.	The First Call Is Yours…
90.	When Your Life…
92.	Better to Die…
94.	If You Stand…
96.	Jesus Paid Your Way…
98.	Better to Give Your…
100.	Jesus Saves Only Those…
102.	If You Give Your Heart…
104.	If Your Hand…
106.	Fear Nothing But…
108.	If You Feel trapped…

110.	Faith Deletes the Word…
112.	The Life You Save…
114.	The Procrastinators' Graduation…
116.	When You Look at a Beggar…
118.	You May Be a Child…
120.	If You Haven't Heard…
122.	Life Is Only Life Until…
124.	When You See the Light
126.	Faith Testing Begins with…
128.	Who in His Right Mind…
130.	If You Believe in Hell…
132.	Heaven Is Full…
134.	You May Never See…
136.	When Temptation Calls…
138.	Your Soul Is the Only Thing…
140.	Extended Life Is Having to Say…
142.	Don't Knock Salvation Until…
144.	If You Sing for the Lord…
146.	Death Is a Fact…
148.	If You Are Not Writing…
150.	Nothing Awaits You in Heaven…
152.	Do You want a New Life…
154.	Would Those Who Do Not Want…
156.	When you give your…

INTRODUCTION

Life Lines has come together as a collection of thoughts related to Christ, Christianity, the cross and salvation, among other related Biblical thoughts, over several decades. It is hoped that one line or another will be that which sparks the individual to look seriously at what the Lord has to offer. For those who already know Christ, the author thinks that they can be sparked to think about creating their own life lines. Each Christian has been drawn (John 4:64) by the Father to Himself through His Son Jesus Christ. Since we are also called to become fishers of men, it is always the right time to go fishing, fishing for souls of men to be sure. Each one of us must cast his/her own life line.

ACKNOWLEDGEMENTS

I acknowledge that Jesus Christ is the Son of God, born of a virgin, sent by the Father to become a blood sacrifice to save the souls of all who would come to believe in Him.

I acknowledge that faith comes by hearing the word of God (Romans 10:17). That all who would come to believe in Him would not perish but would come to inherit eternal life. I acknowledge His healing ministry is still active today and that I have been healed by Him as well as delivered by Him. I have experienced His gift of salvation, His healing touches, seen some of His miraculous works with my own eyes. I have seen many of His nine gifts of the Spirit (if not all) at work in several ministries as well as in our own. I have also witnessed His enemy and my enemy, Satan, at work in modern-day ministries through the evil works of worldly people as well as false Christians. My belief is such that His word as recorded in the Holy Scriptures is the holy, inerrant, infallible word of God. I also acknowledge that what I might not understand clearly since I see as through a glass darkly will be revealed to me in eternity. I understand and believe in God the Father, God the Son, and God the Holy Spirit.

In my secondary acknowledgements, I attribute honour and appreciation to my wife Sarah Ann Mundle and all the greatness that God has bestowed upon her.

I will till the day I die acknowledge that God's grace will grant unto all of our children ample opportunity to be saved and that He has currently returned one and her entire family to the cross of Christ. They currently live a life of practicing Christians. I acknowledge that as a bona fide miracle of God who called them through His Son Jesus Christ.

OTHER CHRISTIAN PUBLICATIONS BY THE AUTHOR

Poetry

Faithwalkers (Christian Poetry) Xlibris
Church What Are You Doing to My Bride (Christian Poetry) Xlibris
Naked Christians (Christian Poetry) Xlibris
The Way of Light (Christian Essays) Xlibris
From the Cradle to the Cross (Christian Poetry) Xlibris

Adult: Spiritual:
Catch the Light Series of Devotionals whose subtitles are listed below.
All had been published by CFP Concepts Inc.

The Valley Walker
While You Have the Light
Let Angels Rejoice
Two Kinds of Light
Where Will You Be in a Thousand Years?

YOUTUBE ADDRESSES FOR THE AUTHOR'S CHRISTIAN SONGS

Multicoloured Soul
https://www.youtube.com/watch?v=YND2CDAZAIU&t=3s

Your Word
https://www.youtube.com/watch?v=aeBBGWYlLWw&t=4s

The Christians are Gone - Fred Mundle - YouTube
https://www.youtube.com/watch?v=RdxFNOU3XUQ

Come Out of Babylon - youtube – Frederick Mundle
https://www.youtube.com/watch?v=-4xFJXXYtco

Apply The Blood - YouTube
https://www.youtube.com/watch?v=0JOLL4JNEm8

I'll Look for You in Paradise
https://www.youtube.com/channel/UCGJzTdskVoVdYe3UOS9f25w

If My People
https://www.youtube.com/watch?v=ltJQwQCv0Hk

The Latter Rain
https://www.youtube.com/watch?v=CLIw1Jzq9MA

NOTE: Type in "youtube" and the title of the song and/or the name: Frederick Mundle

LIFE LINES

FREDERICK MUNDLE

Proverbs 10:4

We all
know where
procrastinators
go!!!

Ephesians 4:26

LET NO SUNSET SEE YOUR ANGER

Titus 3:2

HE WHO SAYS NOTHING NICE ABOUT EVERYBODY SAYS NOTHING NICE ABOUT ANYBODY

Proverbs 16:24

LET
KIND
WORDS
FLY
LIKE
OINTMENT
INTO
TENDER
EARS

Proverbs 20:19 (NIV)

A WAGGING TONGUE FANS FLAMES IN FOOLS

Matthew 9:27-30

If you don't
believe
in miracles,
pluck out
your eyes

Proverbs 19:17

Pity those
who have
as much
as you;
Help those
who don't

Psalms 27:8-9

Step on your hands while you settle your disputes

John 14:2-6

A REAL CARPENTER BUILDS HIS HOUSE IN HEAVEN

Matthew 6:9-13

WHAT YOU BARE ON A PSYCHIATRIST'S COUCH, YOU CAN SAVE ON YOUR KNEES

John 8:7

IF STONES WERE COINS, HOW MANY WOULD YOU THROW?

1 Corinthians 3:15

Philemon 1:6 (ESV)

The early bird spreads the Word

Proverbs 22:6

Every Father wants to see His children in Heaven

Matthew 7:1

WHEN STONES TURN TO FLOWERS, CAST THE FIRST ONE

John 14:6

IF DARWIN WAS SAVED, HE FOUND THE MISSING LINK

John 10:27

ALL
HIS
CHILDREN
KNOW
THAT
THEY
ARE

Ecclesiastes 11:6

Sow
in
the
season
of
the
man

John 11:25-26

Where is Einstein now?

Matthew 4:19

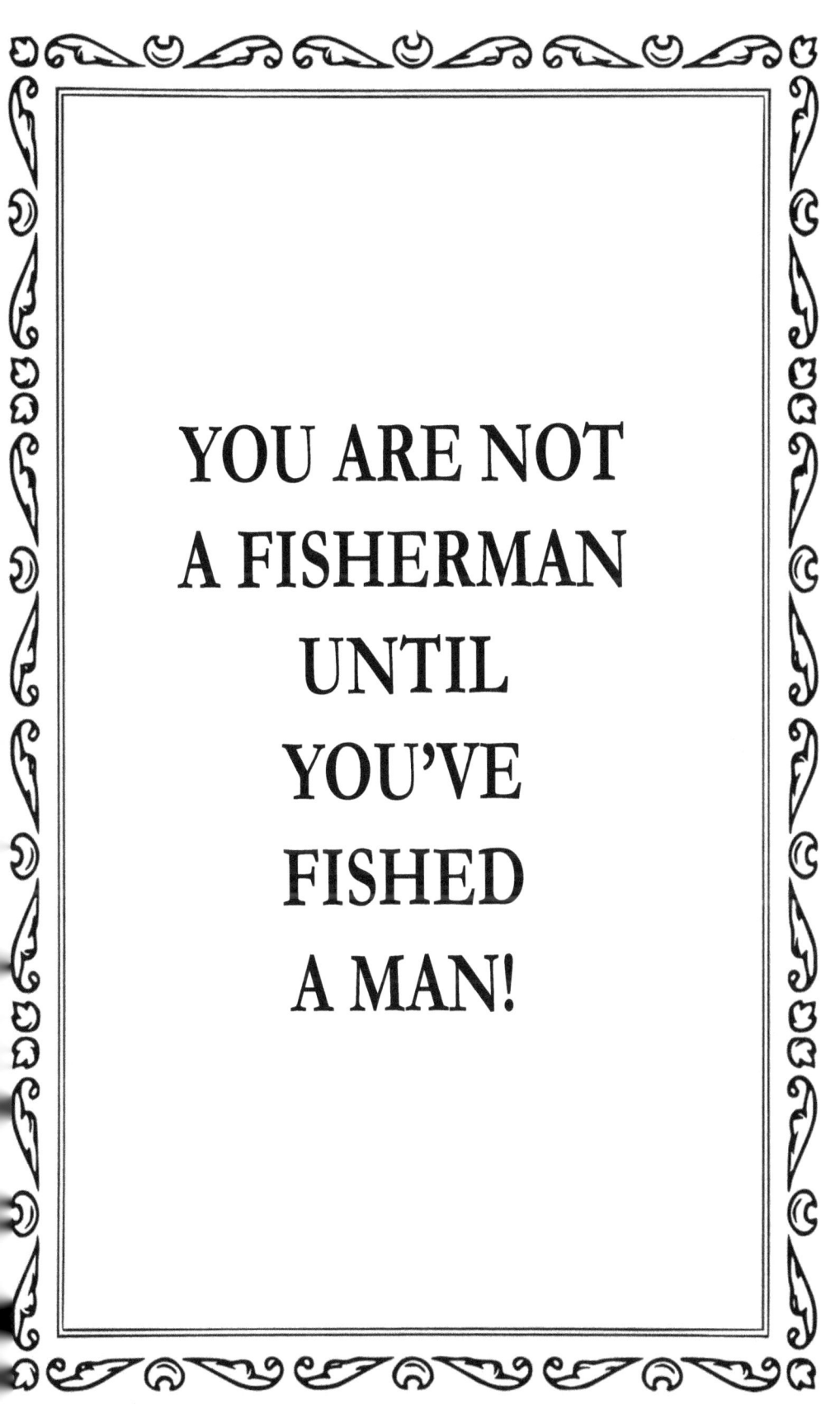

YOU ARE NOT A FISHERMAN UNTIL YOU'VE FISHED A MAN!

James 2:17 (14-26)

If you
can still
count
your works,
you
are
in
trouble

Psalm 53:1

People without God see a *psychiatrist*

Mark 4:14-20

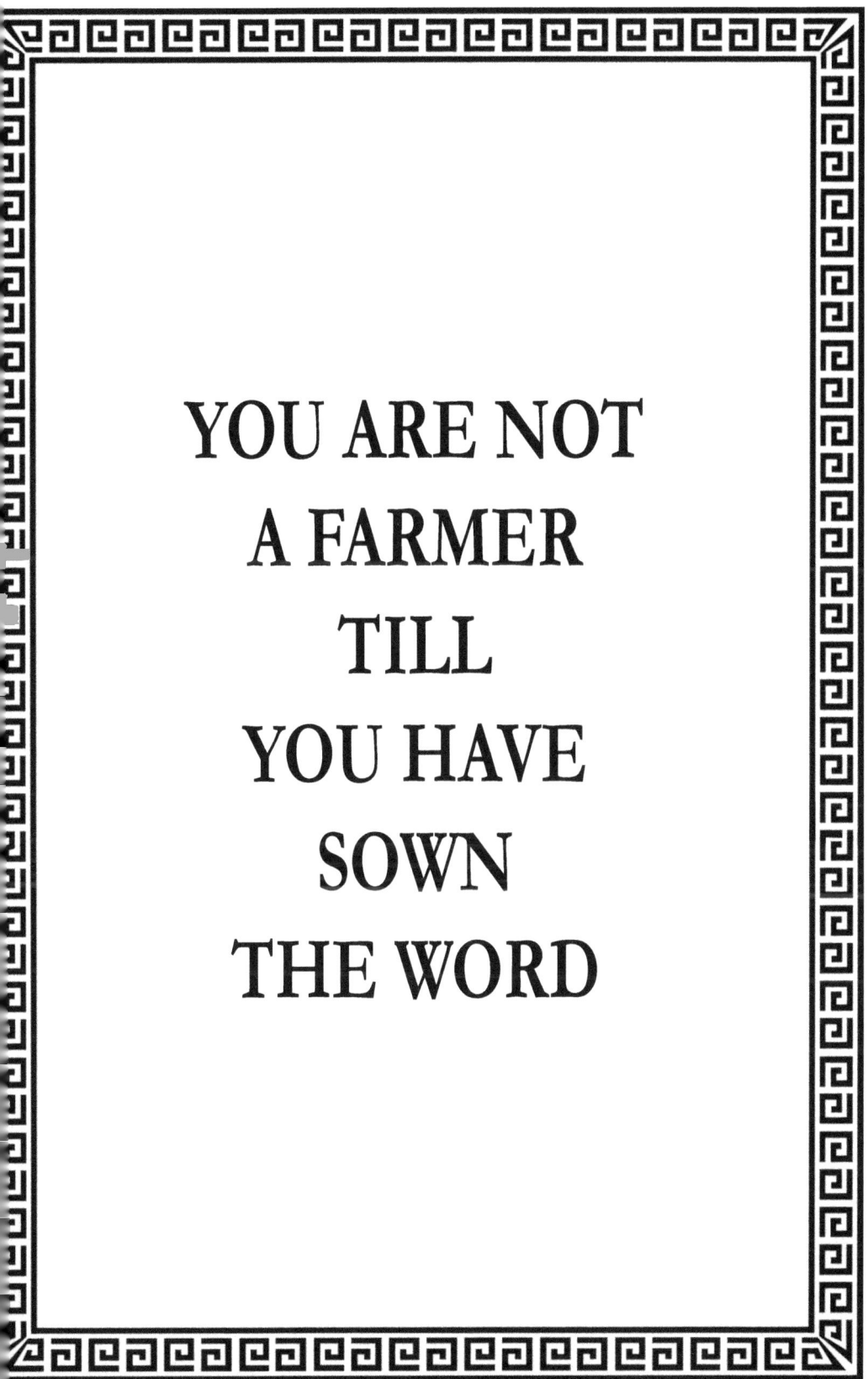

YOU ARE NOT
A FARMER
TILL
YOU HAVE
SOWN
THE WORD

Matthew 21:44

Many a rock
has been broken
by
His Word

John 3:7-8

ONLY A CHRISTIAN IS TWICE BORN: FIRST OF HIS MOTHER, THEN OF HIS FATHER.

Proverbs 15:29 and John 9:31

CHRISTIAN PRAYERS ARE ANSWERED; PAGAN PLEAS UNHEARD

James 1:22

MUTE CHRISTIANS WILL ANSWER TO JESUS

John 3:16

THE PAGAN LIVES FOR TODAY WHEREAS THE CHRISTIAN LIVES FOREVER

Psalm 18:46 (Living Bible)
Luke 24:6-8

Bad news for non Christians: God is alive and well; Jesus is too.

John 3:3

NON CHRISTIANS
HAVE NOTHING
TO LOSE
EXCEPT
ETERNAL LIFE:

BE BORN AGAIN!

John 15:15

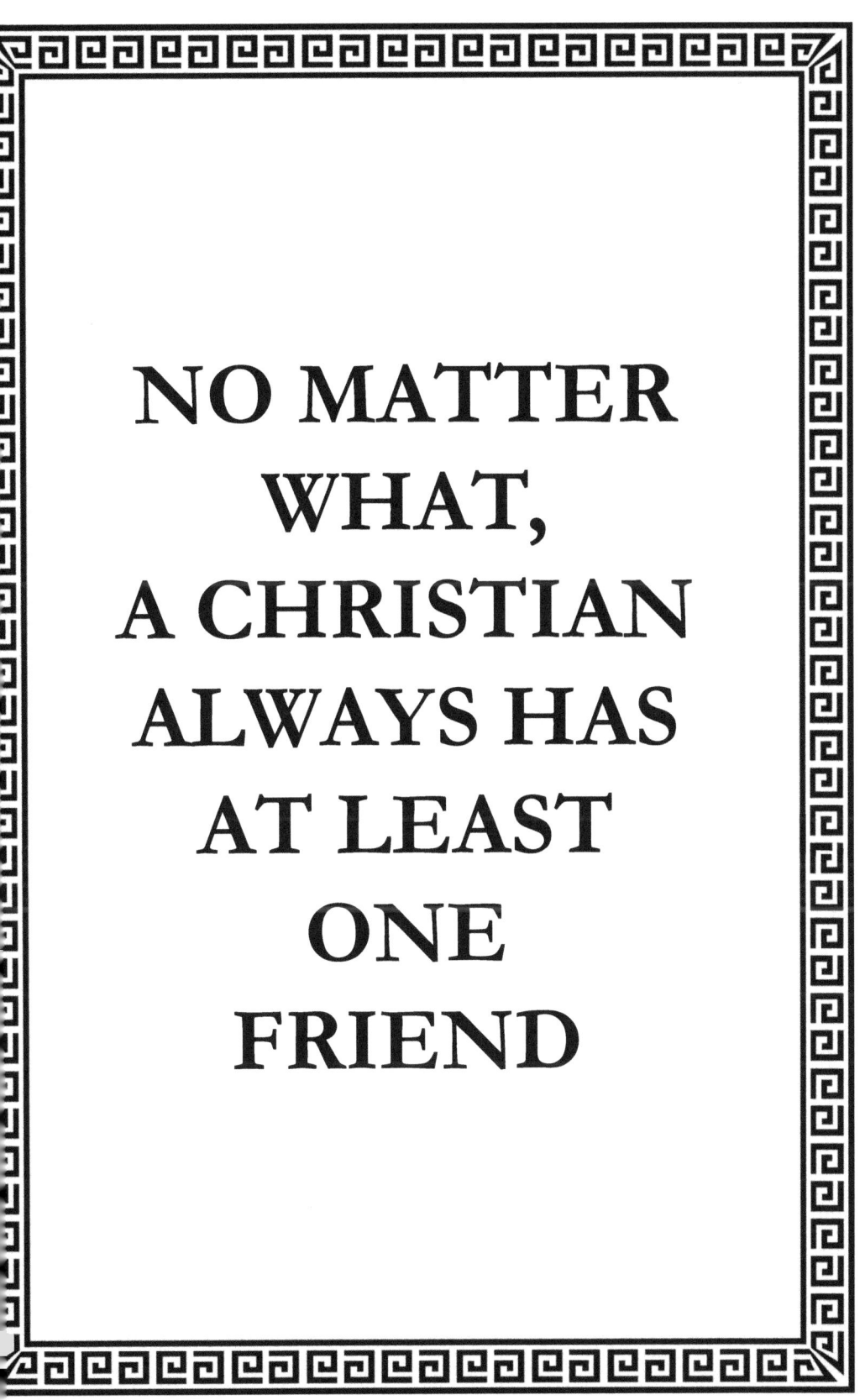

Matthew 5:38-39

A
Christian
has
two
rosy
cheeks

2 Peter 3:13

A CHRISTIAN ALWAYS LOOKS AS THOUGH HE'S GOING SOMEWHERE

2 Timothy 2:1

THE WORLD IS A BOOT CAMP FOR CHRISTIAN SOLDIERS

1 John 2:17

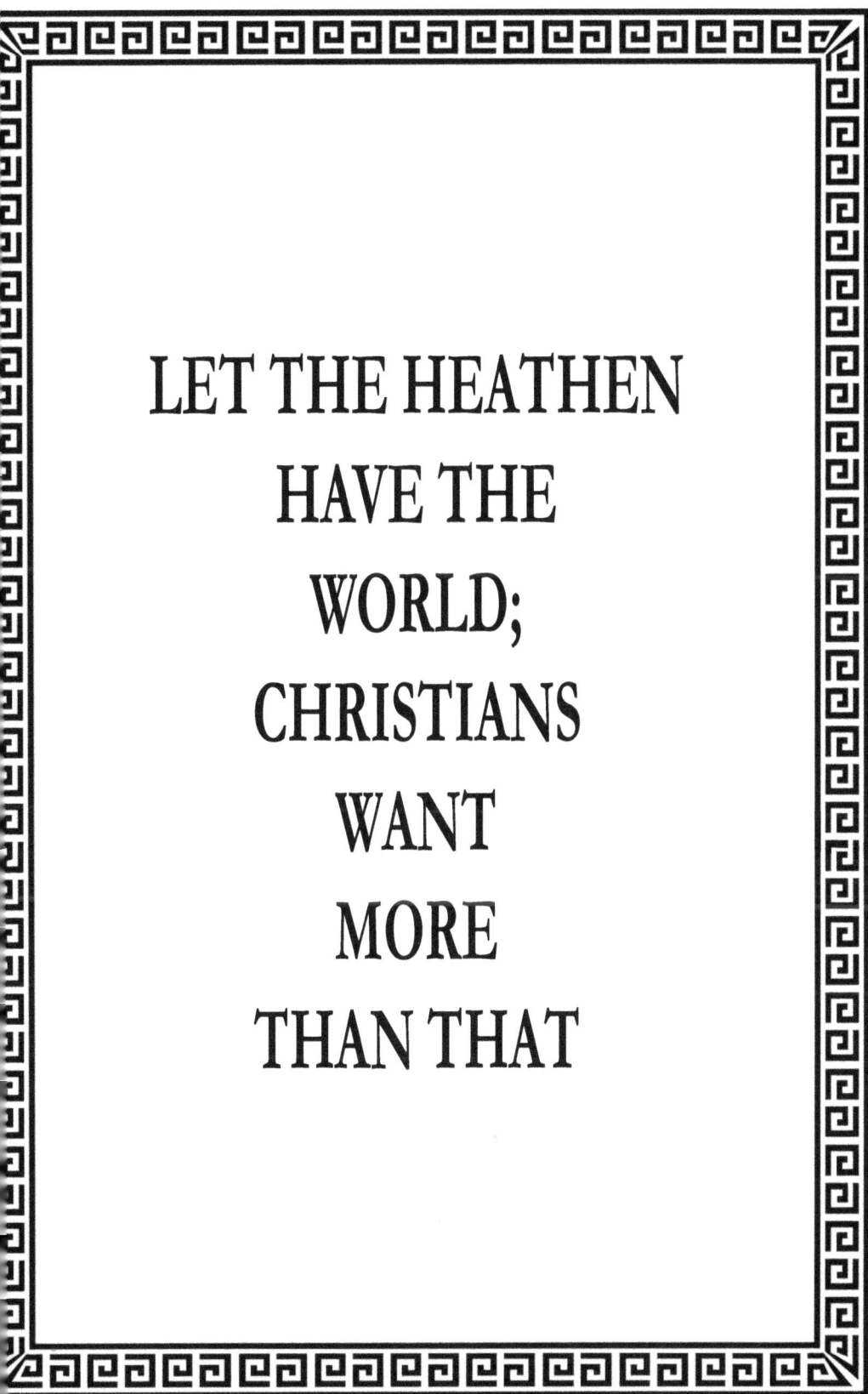

Matthew 6:19-21

Stored treasures
in heaven
are words
for Jesus
on Earth

Matthew 10:32

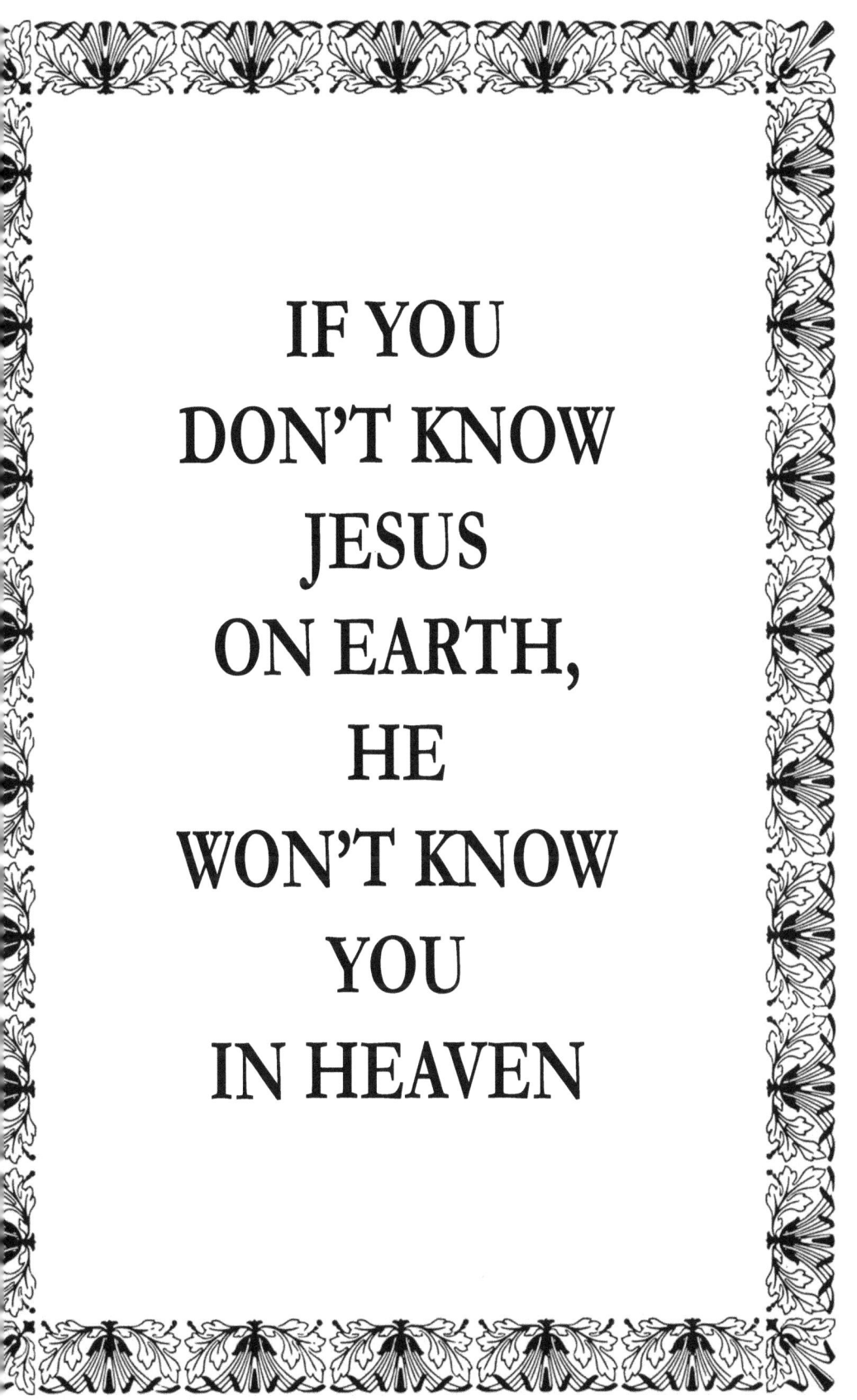

1 Peter 5:7

JESUS
IS
THE
ONLY
SHRINK

Philippians 4:19

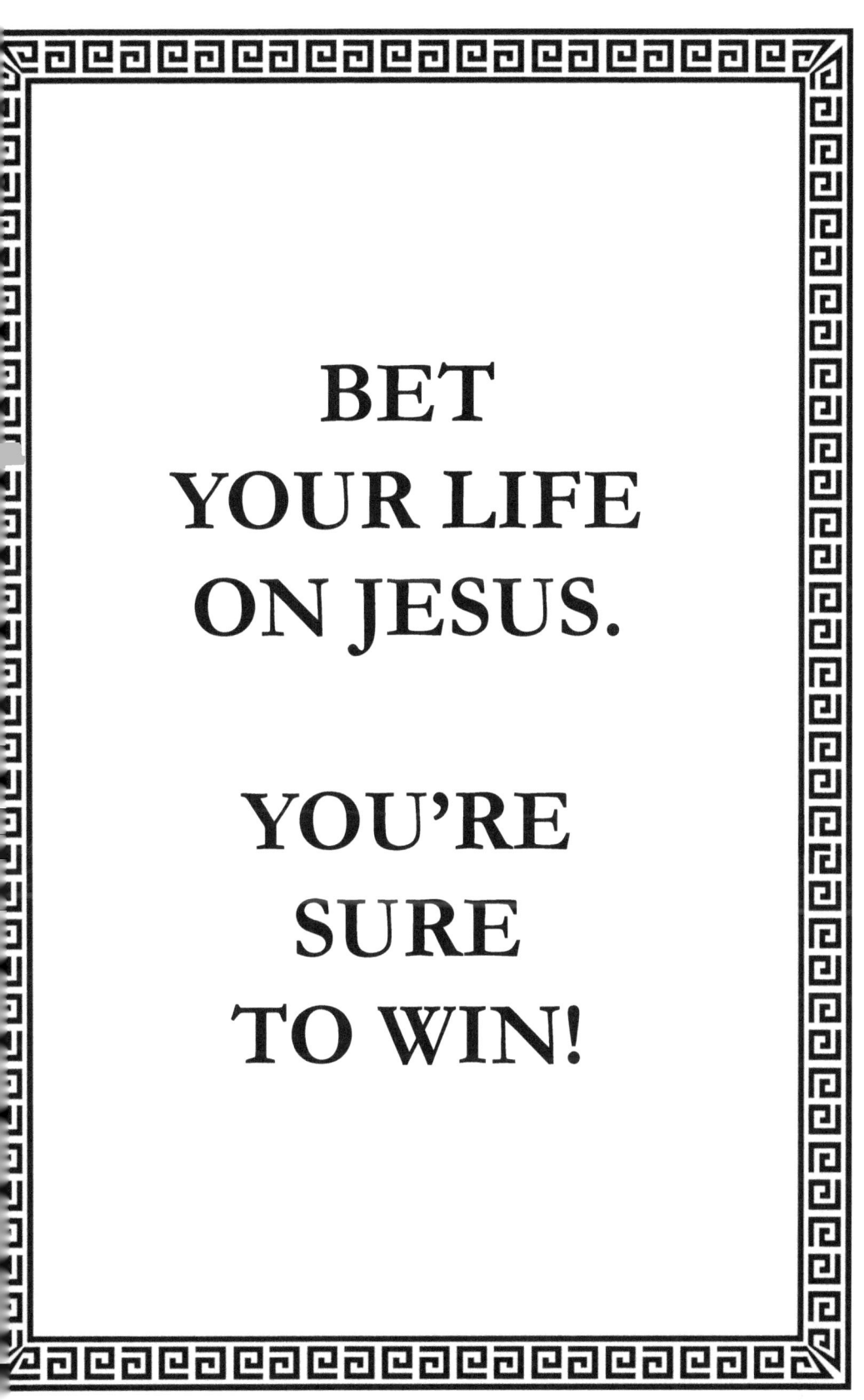

2 Thessalonians 3:10-13

JESUS HIRES ANYBODY
WHO WANTS TO WORK
BUT
SAVES ONLY
THOSE THAT
DO

Matthew 7:21-23

IT'S TOO LATE WHEN JESUS ASKS YOUR NAME

John 8:12

If Jesus
is the light,
why
do you live
in
the dark?

Matthew 22:14

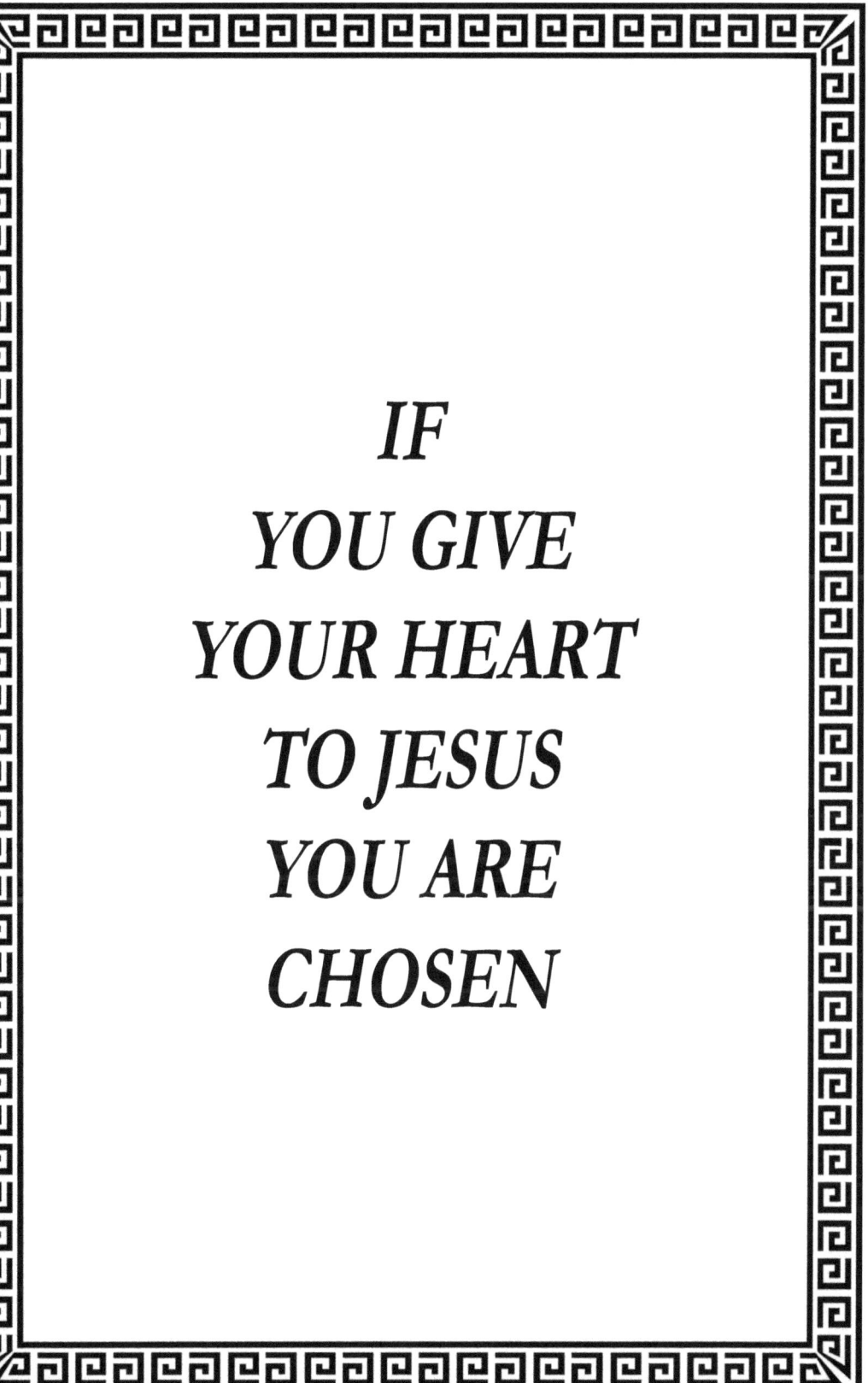

Romans 10:13

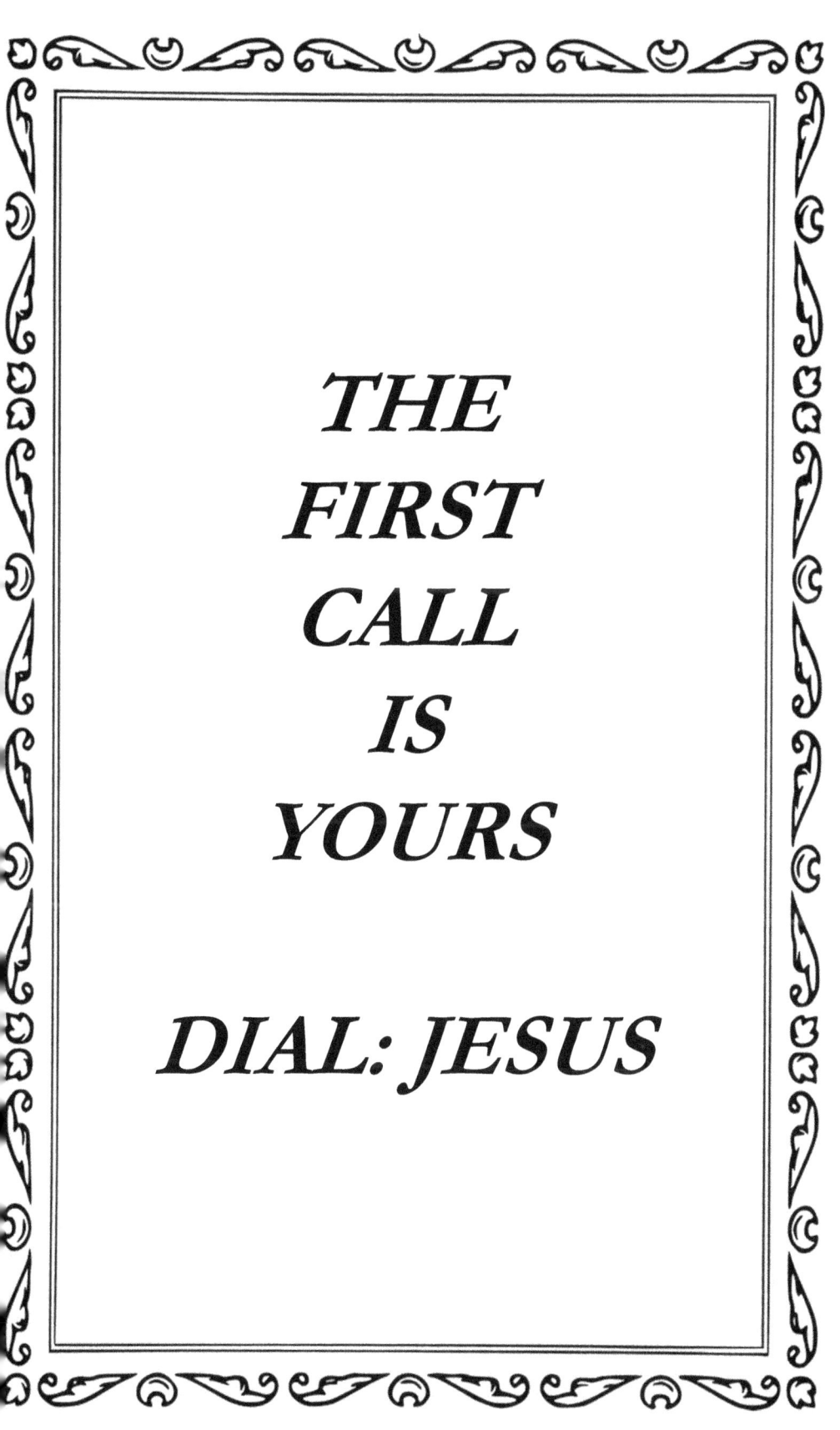

Matthew 11:28-30

When life
gets you
down
let
Jesus
pick you
up

Romans 14:7-9

*Better
to die
for the Lord
than
to live
for the
devil*

Matthew 10:32-33

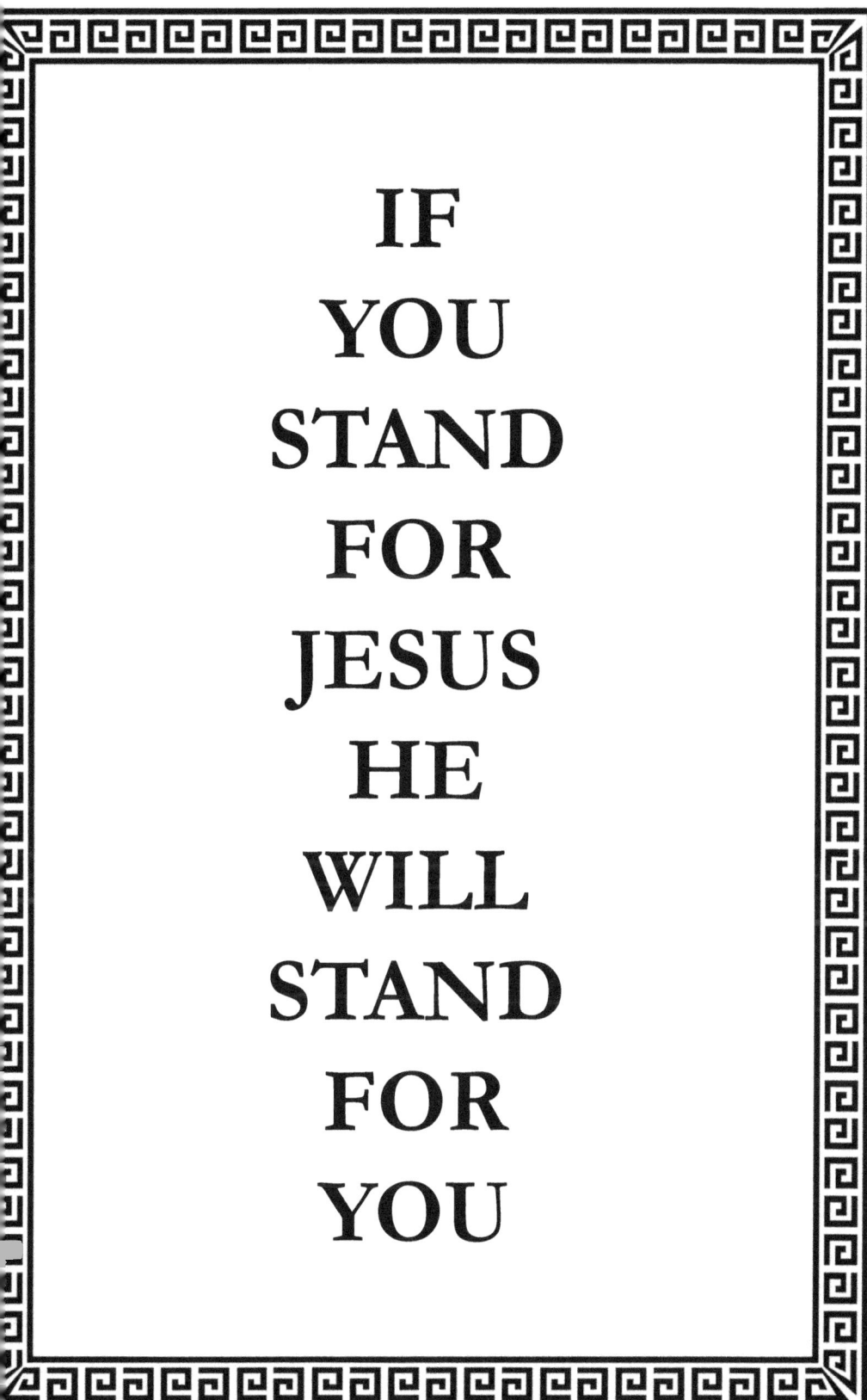

1 John 2:2 and Acts 2:21

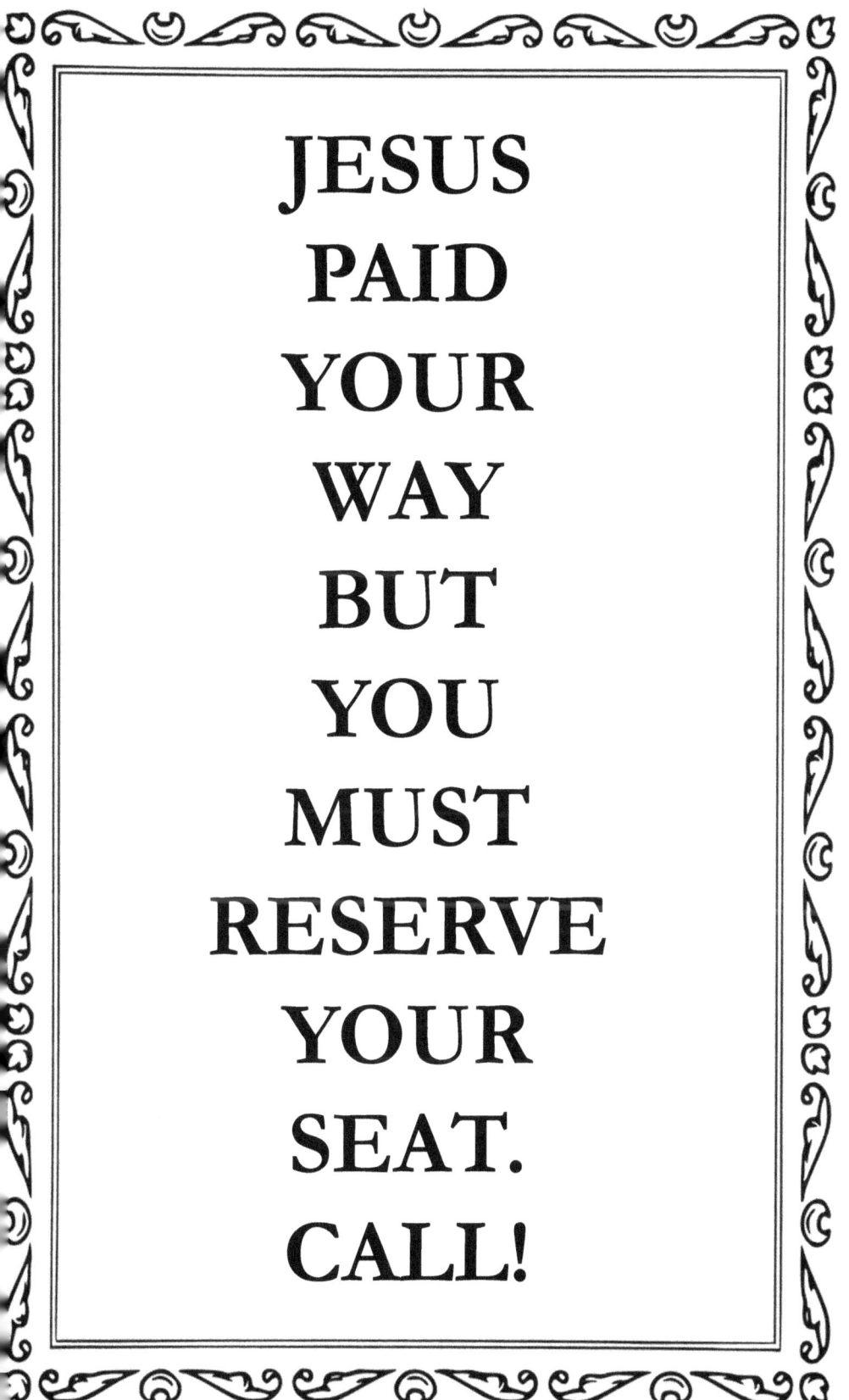

Matthew 16:26

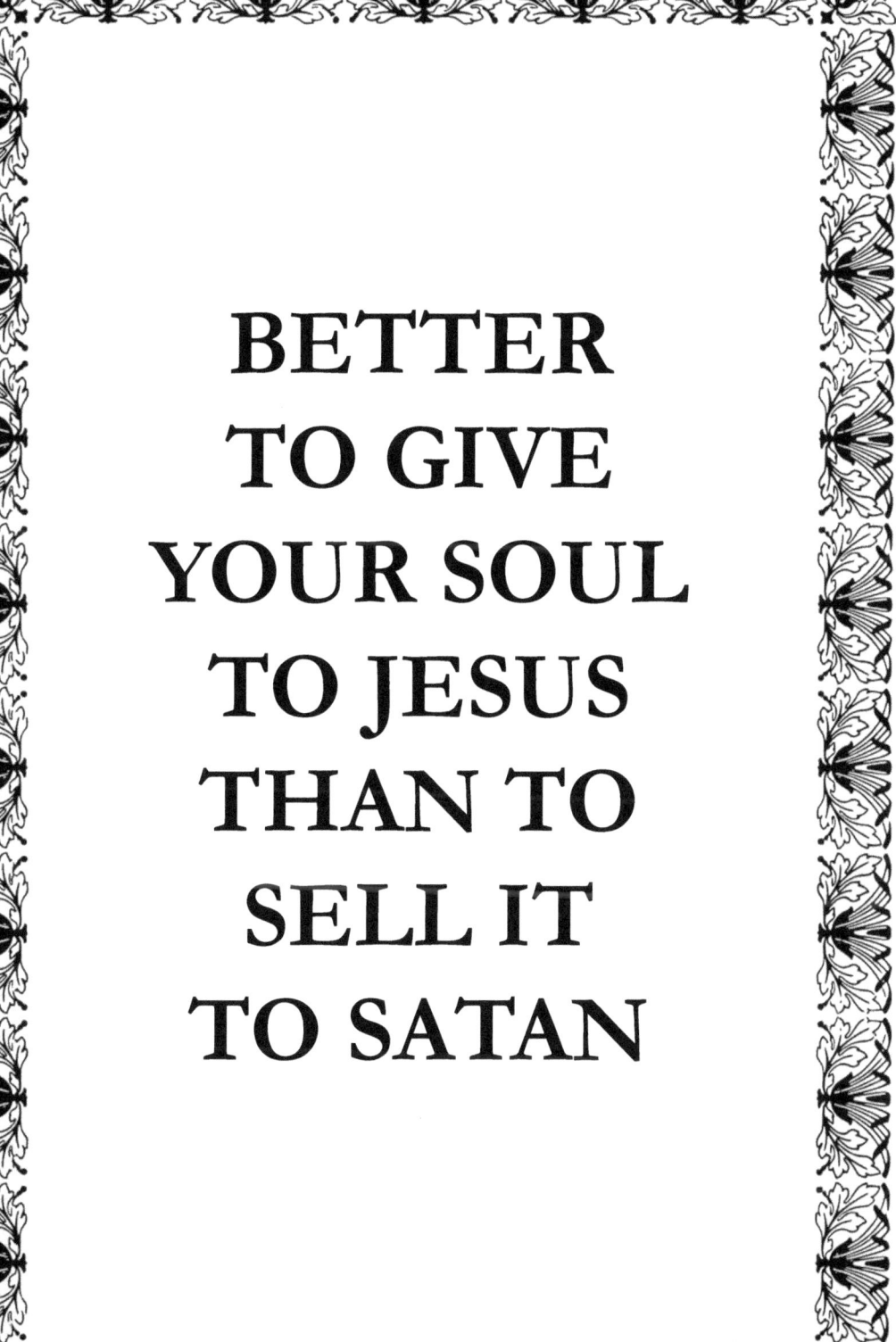

Matthew 19:24-26

JESUS SAVES ONLY THOSE WHO ASK

Job 11:13-19

If you give
your heart
to Jesus,
you are
chosen.
If you don't,
you
have chosen

Matthew 25:40 and Matthew 7:12

If your hand
is moved to give,
the Lord
is nudging you
to help
His children

Romans 12:19 and Romans 13:4

FEAR NOTHING BUT GOD'S WRATH: REPENT!

Matthew 10:28 and Revelation 21:8

IF
YOU FEEL
TRAPPED
ON EARTH,
HOW
WILL
YOU FEEL
IN HELL?

Hebrews 11:6

FAITH DELETES THE WORD "IMPOSSIBLE" FROM THE LORD'S DICTIONARY

James 1:21

THE LIFE YOU SAVE SHOULD BE YOUR OWN!

Luke 9:59-62

THE PROCRASTINATORS'
GRADUATION CLASS
HAS ITS REUNION
IN HELL.
HOPE YOU
MISS IT.

Hebrews 9:27

When you
look
at a beggar,
think
of yourself
on
judgment
day

John 1:12

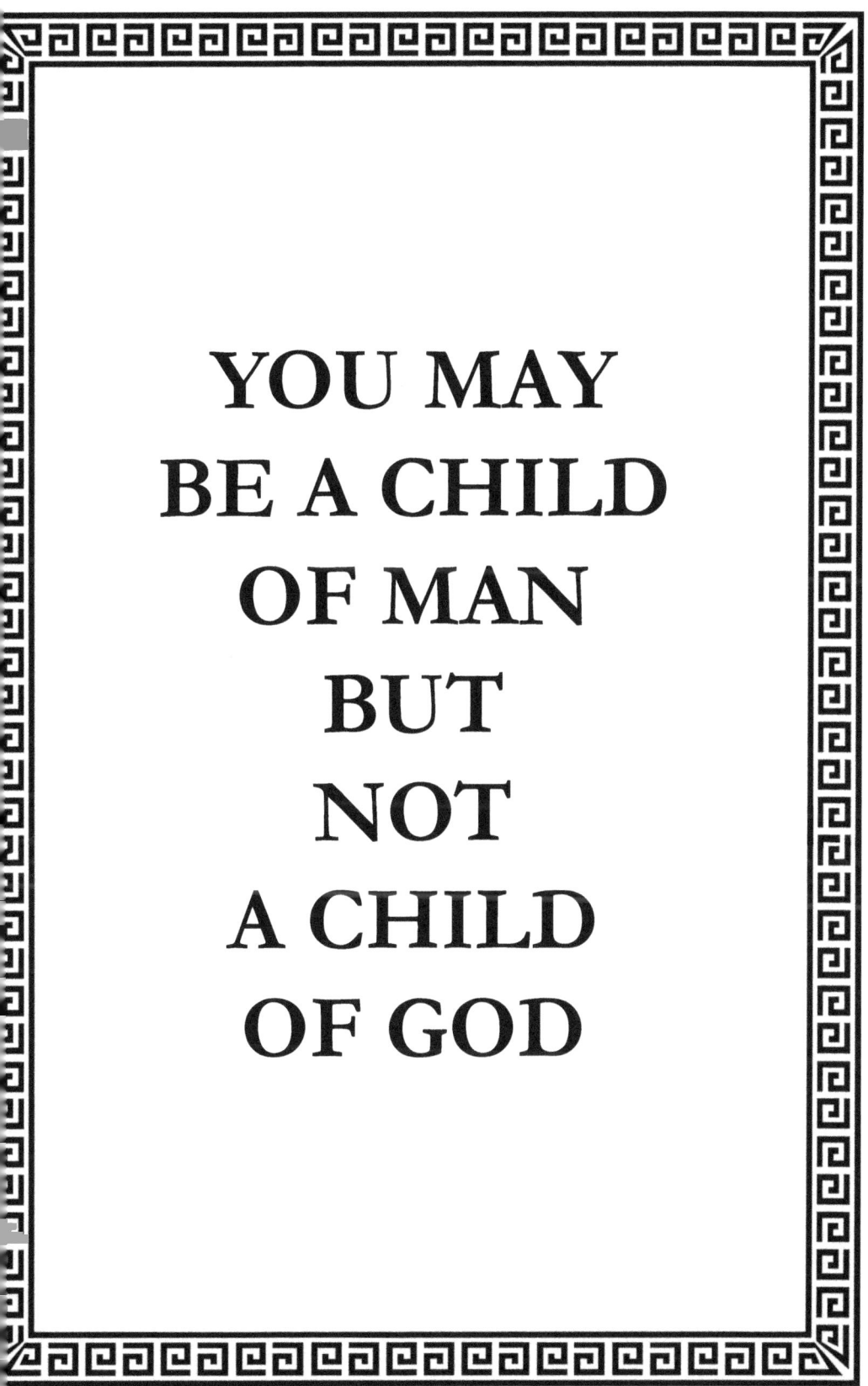

1 Corinthians 15:51-52
1 Thessalonians 4:13-18

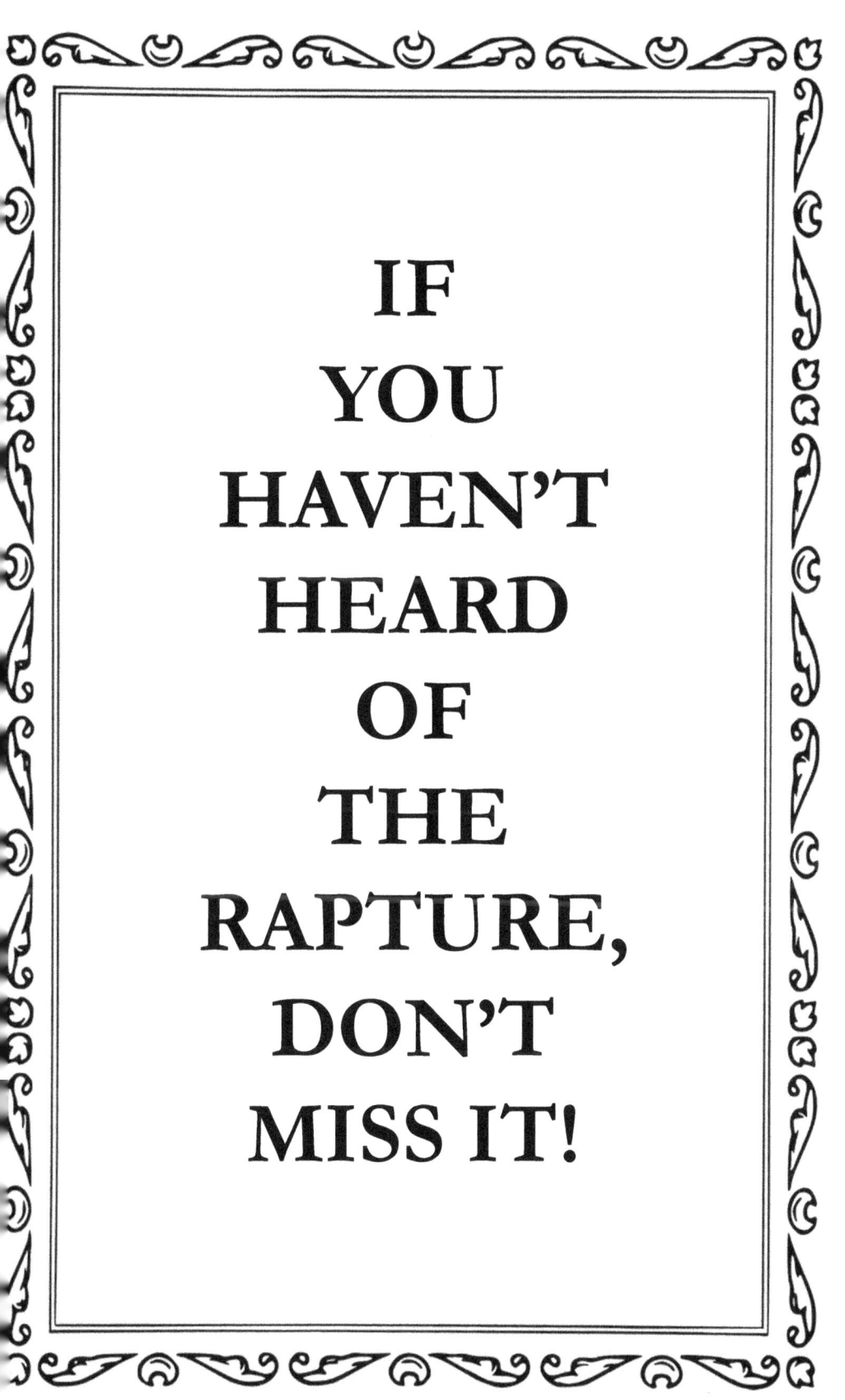

1 John 2:17

LIFE
IS ONLY
LIFE
UNTIL IT IS
EVERLASTING

John 9:5

When you see the *LIGHT* on Earth, know that you are on your way home; When you see the *LIGHT* after you die, know that you are home

James 1:2-4

Faith testing begins with MISFORTUNE

Revelation 2:11 and Revelation 20:6
Revelation 20:14 and Revelation 21:8

WHO IN HIS RIGHT MIND WANTS A SECOND DEATH?

Psalm 9:17 and 2 Thessalonians 1:9 and Mark 9:43

1 Timothy 1:15

HEAVEN IS FULL OF SINNERS

1 John 2:19

YOU MAY NEVER SEE THE "SAVED" AGAIN

Matthew 26:41

WHEN TEMPTATION CALLS, HANG UP!

Mark 8:35-36

Your soul is the only thing worth saving

2 Chronicles 7:14

EXTENDED LIFE IS HAVING TO SAY "I'M SORRY"

Hebrews 7:25

Jeremiah 17:14

If you sing for the Lord on Earth, you will sing for Him in Heaven

Romans 6:22-23

Death
is a fact
of life;
Eternal Life
is a fact
of death
for the saved

Proverbs 3:3

If you are not *writing* for the Lord, you are *freelancing* for the devil.

Matthew 6:19

NOTHING AWAITS YOU IN HEAVEN THAT YOU HAVEN'T PREPARED FOR ON EARTH

John 3:5-8

IF YOU WANT A NEW LIFE, BE BORN AGAIN!

Luke 14:18-20

Romans 14:12 and 1 Peter 4:5

WHEN YOU GIVE YOUR ACCOUNT, PRAY IT'S NOT IN THE RED!

www.ingramcontent.com/pod-product-compliance
Lightning Source LLC
Chambersburg PA
CBHW051547010526
44118CB00022B/2615